Nature Follow-the-Dots Coloring Book

Winky Adam

DOVER PUBLICATIONS INC.
Mineola, New York

Bibliographical Note

Nature Follow-the-Dots Coloring Book is a new work, first published
by Dover Publications, Inc., in 1997.

International Standard Book Number

ISBN-13: 978-0-486-29642-5
ISBN-10: 0-486-29642-3

Manufactured in the United States by Courier Corporation
29642310
www.doverpublications.com

Note

This book is full of fun for anyone who likes nature and who likes connecting the dots! Each of the 56 puzzles is only partly finished; it's up to you to fill in the rest of the picture and discover what it depicts. First, read the hint or question under each puzzle. Then, using a pencil or a pen, start at dot number 1 and draw a line to dot number 2, and then to number 3, and so on. Can you guess what the picture shows before all the dots are connected? There is a list of solutions at the back of the book in case you are having trouble. When all the dots are connected, go back to the beginning and color the pictures in any way you want to. Are you ready? Follow the dots!

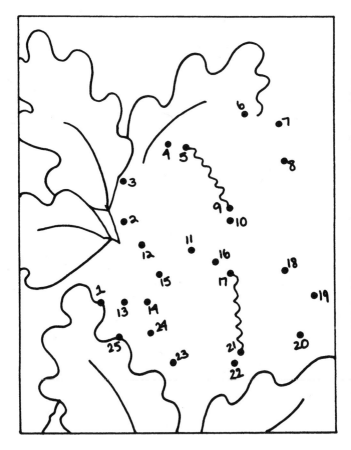

We're often found near oak trees.

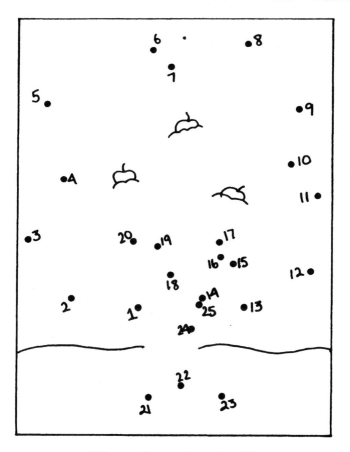

What is that in the orchard?

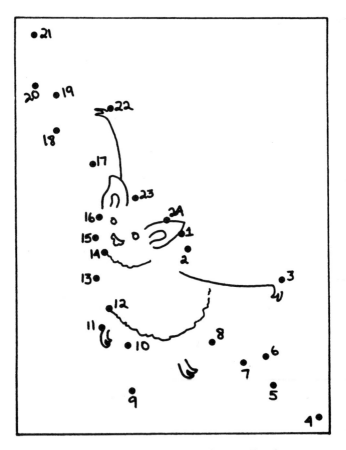

You won't see me flying during the day.

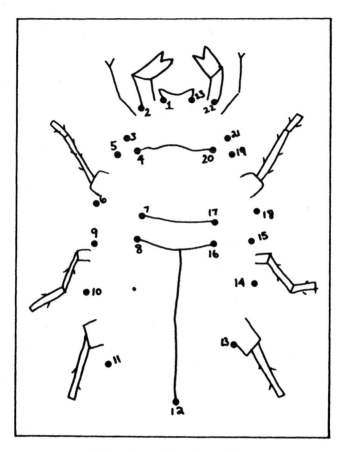

I live beneath rocks and logs.

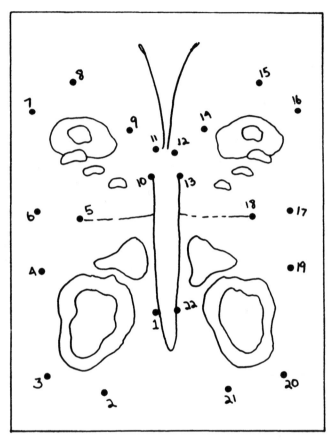

What is this pretty insect?

What makes shade in the desert?

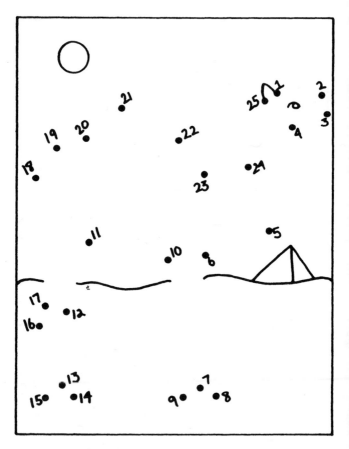

Who can go for days without water?

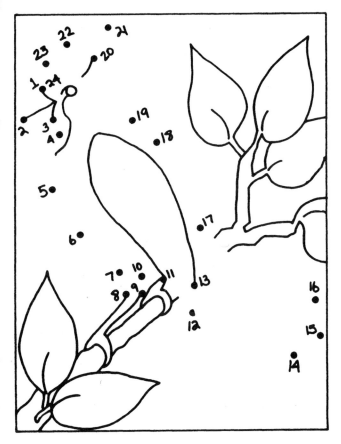

Who has a bright red coat?

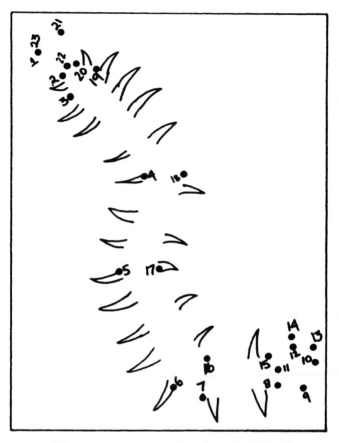

Whose name means "one hundred feet"?

This could have a silver lining.

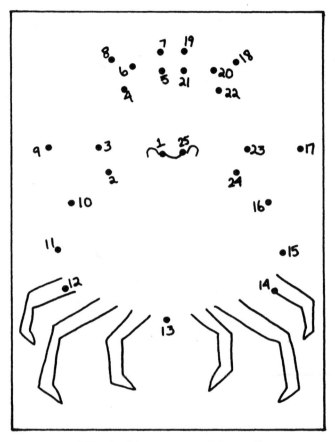

Who is this creature of the sea?

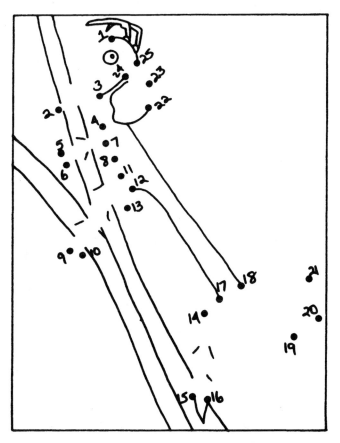

Who chirps in the grass at night?

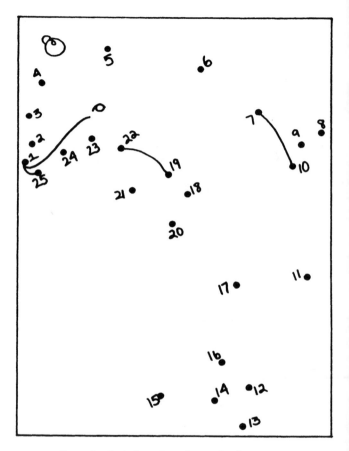

Somebody is leaping through the water.

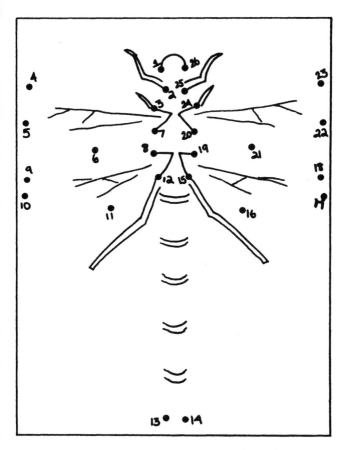

You'll see me near swamps and ponds.

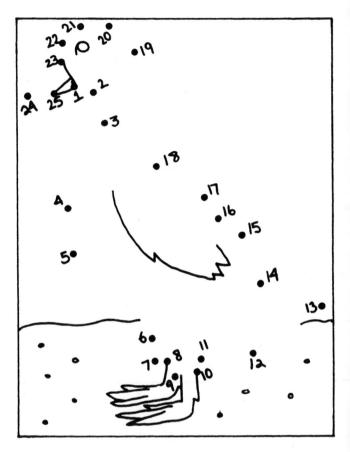

I like to waddle around the farmyard.

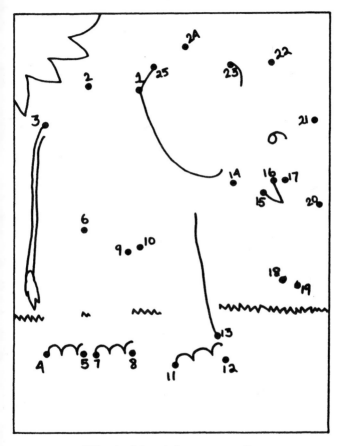

Who is this mighty creature?

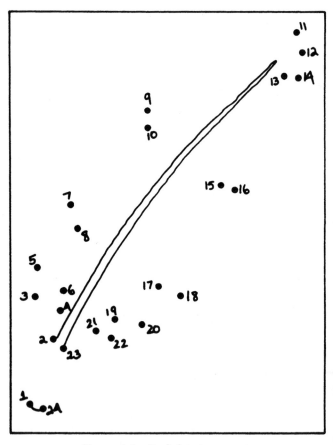

You might find this in a nest.

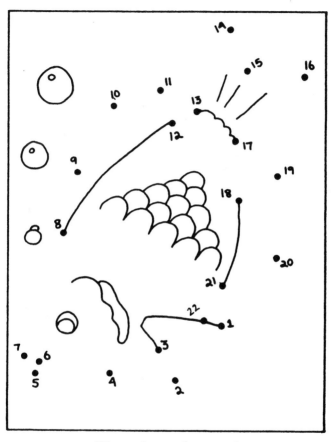

Who is that in the water?

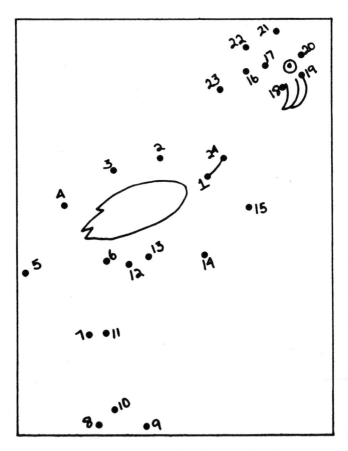

This long-legged fellow lives in Florida.

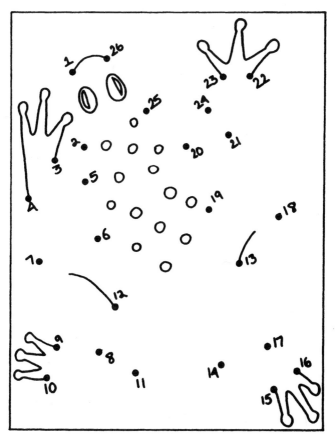

Who is this croaker?

Someone is eating the highest leaves.

24

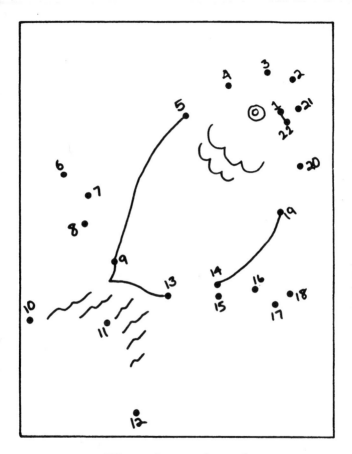

What is this popular pet?

Who is that in the tree?

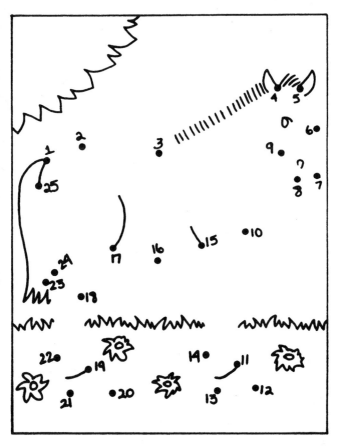

Who is standing in the meadow?

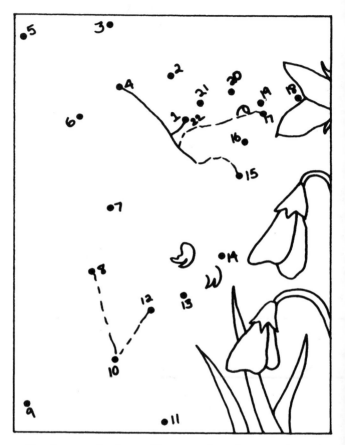

You have to look quickly to catch a glimpse of me.

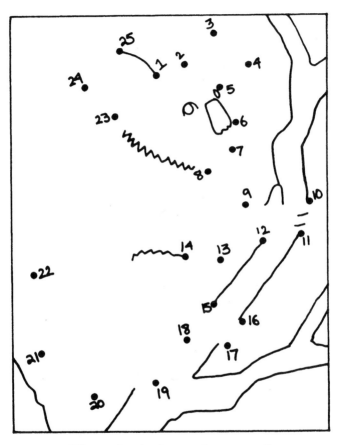

Who is that in the eucalyptus tree?

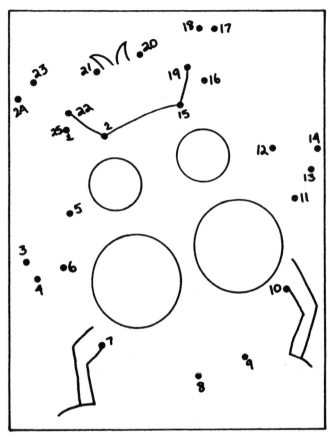

Can you spot what I am?

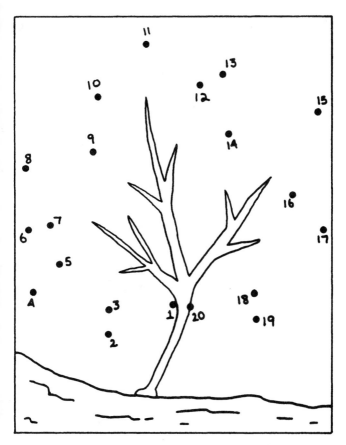

What changes colors as the year goes by?

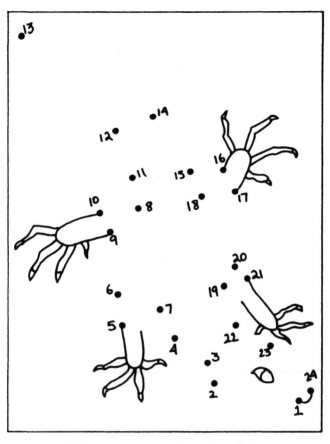

Who runs over rocks and walls?

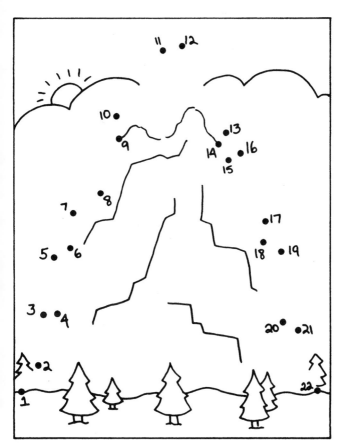

What is bigger than a tree?

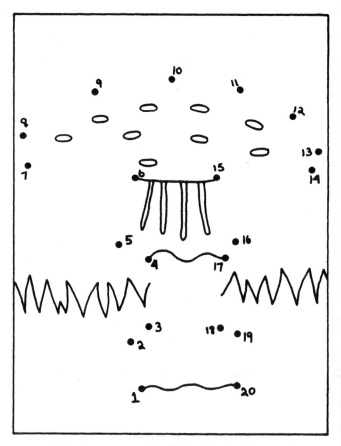

Though very small, this still takes "room."

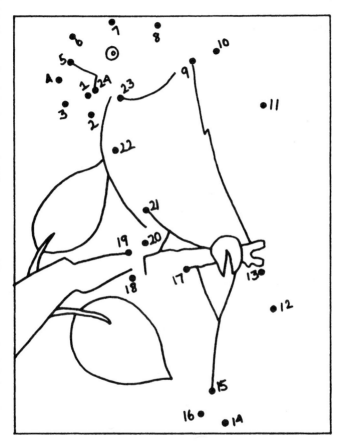

Who is this talkative fellow?

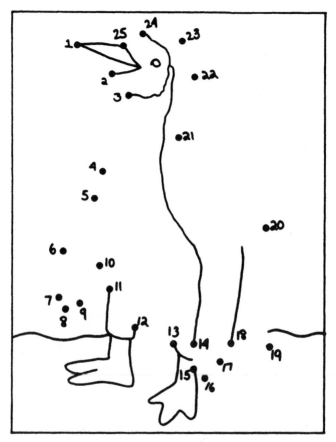

Someone loves the ice and snow.

Who's got a prickly coat?

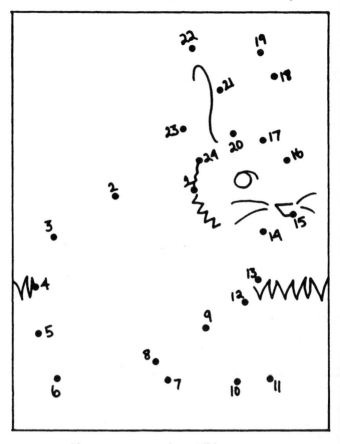

If you come too close I'll hop away.

Somebody is up to greet the dawn.

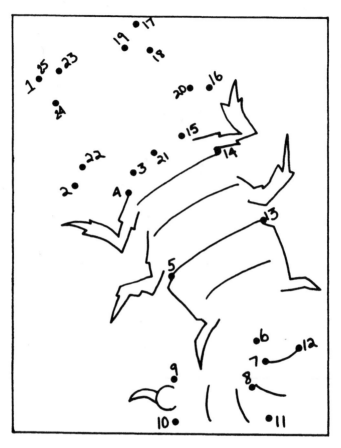

I've got a stinger on my tail.

You'll see me at the beach.

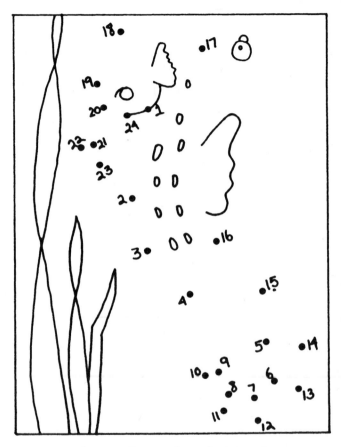

Who is galloping through the sea?

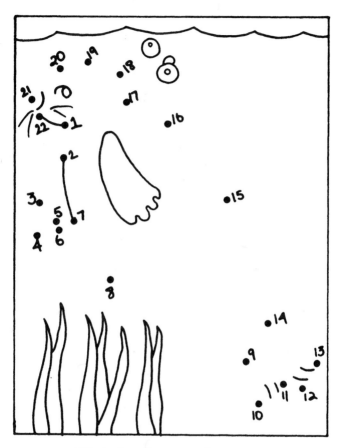

Who's that playing in the water?

What grows on the ocean floor?

Watch out for my teeth!

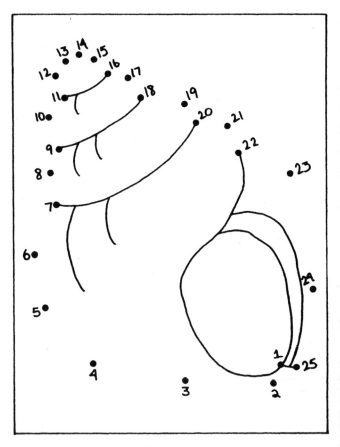

Listen to me and you might hear the sea.

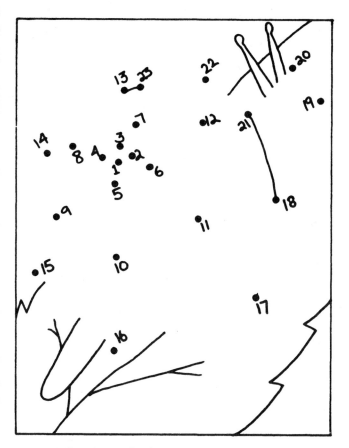

When I travel, I bring my house with me.

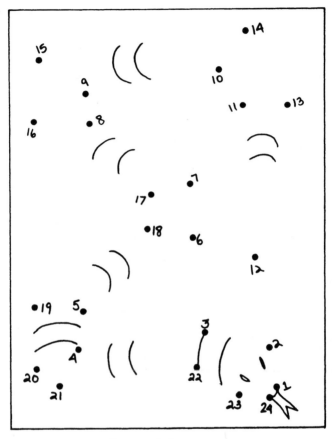

I am a slithery sort.

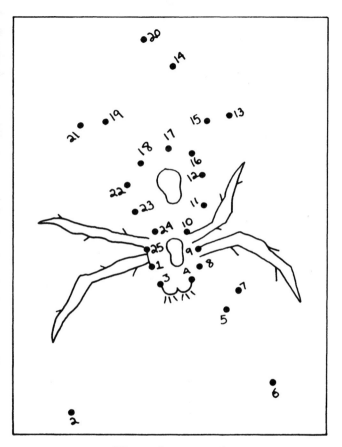

Who is this weaver?

Who is eating the nuts?

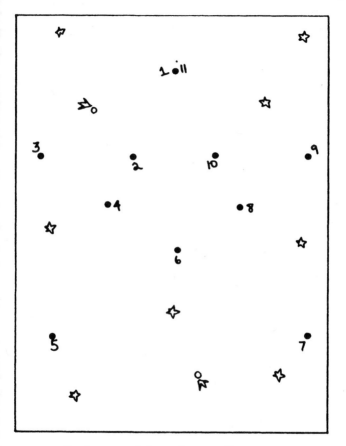

Look up at night and you will see me.

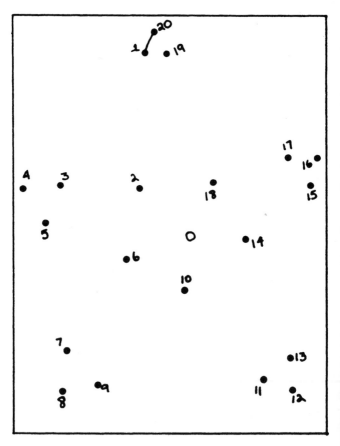

You might see me on the ocean floor.

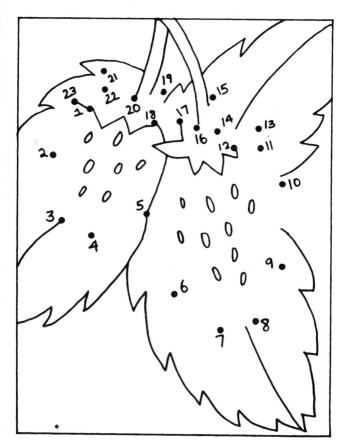

What are these tasty things?

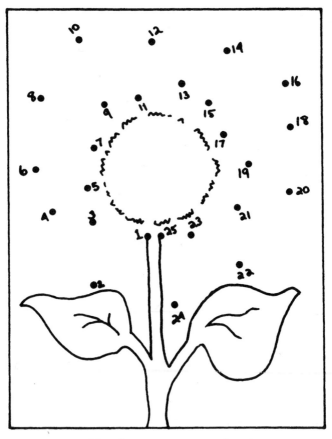

I brighten up many gardens.

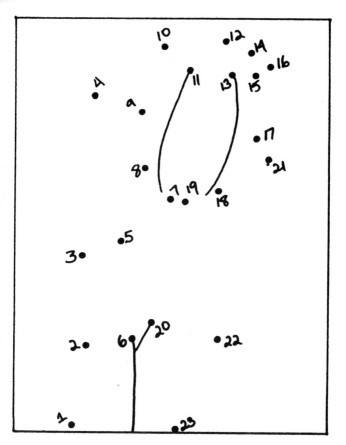

You might see me in Holland.

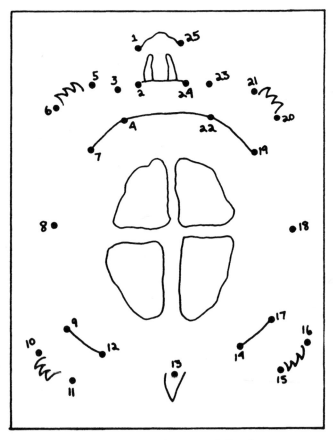

Some people think I'm awfully slow.

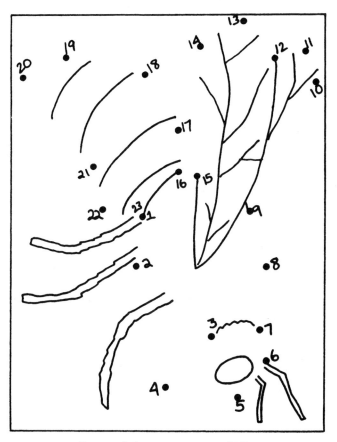

Be careful not to get me mad!

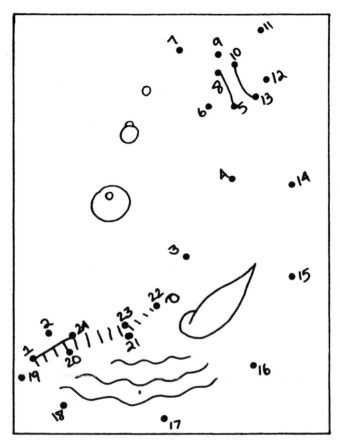

Who's blowing bubbles?

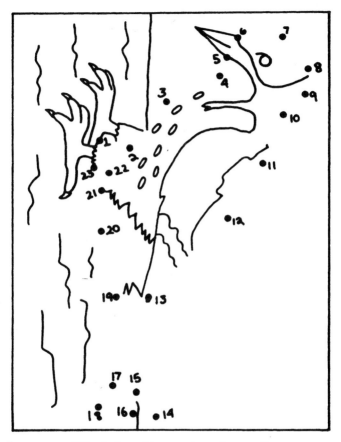

Who is knocking against the tree?

Identifying the Pictures
When you follow the dots, these are what you will find.